My Life

B4&After

Entertainment

Written by Marlon L. Underwood

© Copyright Marlon L. Underwood 2018

All rights reserved. In accordance with the U.S. Copyright Act of 1976, the scanning, uploading, copying and/or electronic sharing of any part of this book without written permission is unlawful piracy. If you would like to use material from this book, (other than for review purposes) prior written permission must be obtained by Marlon L. Underwood.
ISBN: 978-0-578-21130-5

Dedication

This book is dedicated to my Daughter, Mahiah E. Underwood.

Acknowledgments

I could not have written this book or achieved the success in my life without these people being involved in my life: My Mom, Virginia Underwood; Ex-Wife, Vatina; Mary Colbert; my Father and Brother John and Johnny Underwood; my Brothers and Sisters Melody, Cecil, Dwight, Jimmy, Charlie, Ricky, Angel, and Tina. My Nephews Donte' and Charlie Mac. "R.D." my Primary at FMC Lexington. Special thanks to Tavetta Patterson, Mike Valentino, Jerome Lynch and Alfred Adams, Jr.

Last, but certainly not least, I am thankful for the one woman who supported me every day in the Feds and stood by my side for five years waiting for me to come home, my Fiancé, Regina Earvin.

Orlando, Florida 2002

"I can't help feeling as though this is all a dream!" I said to my wife, Vatina, paraphrasing a verse from one of my favorite Rap artists who is no longer among us. Yet, this was certainly no dream. In fact, it was 'my' reality I had to remind myself as I gave her left hand a gentle squeeze.

I did not have to turn my attention to my three sisters, Angel, Melody and Tina, to know that they were extremely proud of my accomplishments!

"I assure you, my love, everything about this moment is real," my wife reassured me with a smile, before bringing my hand to her lips and planting a kiss. Our exchange of words was discrete, so as not to interrupt the pair who were hosting the event.

Although we weren't facing one another, I knew my wife well; therefore I knew her response was followed by a grin. As for me, it took all my strength not to let out a laugh...

Vatina was not only the woman to whom I made a vow before God to honor and protect, she was also my best friend. In fact, she brought such incredible balance to my life. Most people would be extremely nervous leading up to their acceptance speech in front of thousands of attendees, yet there I was smiling, flirting and laughing with my wife, whom God had blessed me with four years prior.

"I wish my mother could have accompanied us on this trip," I found myself whispering to my wife. "Me too," Vatina agreed. "But, I certainly believed her when she hugged you and said that although she couldn't attend, she'd certainly be with you in spirit." My wife was reminding me of the conversation my mother and I had prior to our departure for Florida, which by now had become indelibly etched in my mind.

Although my mother, Virginia Underwood, remained physically hundreds of miles away in Gary, Indiana, I felt as though she was right there beside me. Not to mention, I grew up in a very devout religious household. Most of my family was Jehovah's Witness.

There are times in which I honestly feel as though my belief and dedication to my Faith, despite the bad choices I made years later, play an integral role regarding the favor and blessings that have been bestowed on me.

One of those blessings was American Income Life, the company I worked for that was honoring me for such an outstanding job performance (not to mention, I'd broken every sales record to date at American Income Life). It was obvious to my wife, my three sisters and me, that the company spared no expense as far as we were concerned on this trip to Orlando. I'm talking Five-Star hotels, Five-Star restaurants, Chauffeur-driven limousines, live stage shows – the full-blown Red Carpet treatment! So yes, a part of me still wished that my mother (who was also deathly afraid of flying!) could have attended.

Nevertheless, a man could certainly get used to this VIP lifestyle, I couldn't help thinking to myself with a smile.

"I can only imagine what you are feeling." My wife's words brought me out of my reverie.

Thus far, seeing others taking to the stage to accept their awards and/or give speeches pertaining to their respective branches and Insurance Companies had mostly been a big blur to me.

"However, as much as I appreciate these folks honoring you for what you have brought to and done for 'their' company, I need you to keep God first in everything that you do and/or take on because the sky is certainly the limit for you, Marlon Underwood." Although Vatina spoke barely above a whisper, her words of wisdom would have a profound impact on me.....until this day. That being said, the blur was no more, since it was now my turn to take to the stage!

I began my acceptance speech, making eye contact with my wife before taking in the hundreds of faces in the audience. All of whom, were giving me their full attention!

"I am a native of Gary, Indiana. Yes, the same city and state in which the king of pop music hails from." I paused briefly, as several members of the audience gave applause to the legendary Michael Jackson's success.

"However, the fact that I stand here before you all today, being not only acknowledged but actually 'honored' by one of the biggest, greatest, and most important industries in the world!"

The entire audience was on their feet giving applause, and probably didn't even hear when I added, "Is an indication that there are 'other' shining stars hailing out of Gary, Indiana!"

As I waited for the applause to subside, I made eye contact with each of my three sisters. Tina and Melody stood teary eyed as they applauded. I noticed that my sister Angel simply gave a nod, followed by a wink of the eye as if to say, "I know that's right!"

"In fact, it seems like it was only yesterday that a man by the name of Brian appeared at my front door trying to sell my wife and I some insurance. Growing up Jehovah's Witness I knew first-hand what it felt like to have doors closed in your face, or folks giving their partial attention. Therefore, not speaking for my wife, I decided to give Brian my undivided attention."

Vatina smiled at the memory, several members of the audience gave applause. "Never would I have imagined that my initial encounter with Brian and American Income Life Insurance would not only have a profound impact on my life, but it would change my life forever. Nor could I help critiquing Brian's sales pitch that day."

"Although his pitch was quite impressive, I began to express some of what I would do differently had it been me selling insurance." Again, several members of the audience found humor in my words and laughed even though I was being truthful. "In fact, he and I must have conversed for over an hour! Our conversation regarding insurance ventured into some of my background, previous endeavors and so on. He was so impressed by what all I revealed about myself and my overall point of view, he decided that he'd much rather have me as a member of his American Income Life team, rather than me simply being a customer." On that note, a majority of the audience stood and applauded.

"As a proud member of the American Income Life family," I continued, turning my attention toward Scott (the State General Agent), and Bob (the Regional Agent), both of whom, along with their spouses, were seated next to each other in the front row. "I am truly thankful for the knowledge, opportunities, relationships and treatment that I have learned, established, and received since coming on board."

"In return, I can assure you all at American Income Life as well as my peers in the insurance community that this Award is only the tip of the iceberg. I certainly intend to apply all I have learned thus far in my endeavors to take this wonderful business to the next level in 2003!" The entire audience erupted in cheers and applause!

Making eye contact with my Supervisor, Scott, I could tell that he was thoroughly impressed with my acceptance speech. However, I could only imagine the audience's response had I revealed or expounded on my "48 Laws of Sales".....which unbeknownst to the insurance world had everything to do with 'why' I found myself receiving such a high honor! I smiled inwardly at the thought.

My Life

B4&After

Entertainment

I was born October 13, 1973 in Gary, Indiana to Virginia and John Underwood; I am number eight of ten children, six brothers and three sisters.

My dad was a very intelligent and hard-working man who held a position in the Post Office as an Engineer. He owned the Underwood Pest Control business in Gary, Indiana and sold fish dinners on the weekends at the VFW.

My father is one of the investors who helped the Jackson 5 get their start in the music business. Marcus Fairchild was the manager of the Jackson 5 at the time that my dad was giving money for their travel and shows.

Most people don't know it, but the Jacksons stayed in the building under my Uncle, Joe Underwood before they moved to 2300 Jackson Street in Gary, Indiana. I got my name from Marlon Jackson because my sister Melody was friends with him and liked his name so she named me Marlon Leon Underwood. My mom is a very sweet and loving woman who loves all her children. My mom is also a very devout Jehovah's Witness in the Christian congregation.

I learned a lot from both of my parents. I learned from my dad to strive for the best in life and to work hard for what I wanted. I learned from my mom the value of being a lovable person and to treat others the way I wanted to be treated.

I took those values to school with me and I excelled. Starting in elementary school I won a pride oratorical contest where all the students from 3rd grade to the 6th grade wrote an essay on pride and "what it meant to you." As a result of winning the contest, my picture and the essay that I wrote was in the newspaper. I stayed on the honor roll every year and eventually I was invited to City Hall to introduce Mayor Richard Gordon Hatcher to the media. I did this standing on a chair at the podium because I was too short.

During the meeting at City Hall I spoke from my heart using all the skills I learned from going to the Kingdom Hall, such as good eye contact, modulation and a commanding tone of voice. It was at that time I learned that I was different and I had something special that many people liked. While I excelled in school I also went to the Christian meetings with my mom.

It was there that I learned public speaking at the young age of eight. Public speaking was taught to all the youth in the congregation. It was there, I believe that I learned the foundation to understanding how to be the greatest salesman on earth today.

At the age of 10, I met an awesome girl in school, her name is Regina Earvin. She was built like a grown woman at a young age. Every guy at school was after her so I just observed her from a distance and admired her beauty. I was quite serious about my education but at the same time I used my gift of public speaking to attract girls. I noticed that whenever I opened my mouth everyone listened to what I said. I was a short guy with a beautiful smile and because of this gift I have a lot of friends and a lot of the guys liked being around me.

My mom said that I was the leader out of all my friends and they would do whatever I told them to do. The elementary school recognized how everyone would cling to me and at the end of the school year they gave me an award called "Mr. Congeniality." I was friends with all the troubled kids, gangsters, honor students and the outcasts in our school. I was just being me, the lovable person my mom taught me to be as a child. This quality made me a special person and I was well loved by all the people who came into contact with me. After graduating from elementary school I went to Pulaski Middle School, where I continued to excel in my education and I stayed on the honor roll.

I had my first real relationship with a girl named Camille; she was a short Puerto Rican and Black female who was very beautiful. She was crazy about me and loved calling and talking on the phone when we were not in school. I remember walking her home and the whole school would follow us to her house on Louisiana Street in Gary to see us kiss before she went inside. I walked her home from school for months. On the way back, walking to my house I met a young lady named Lucrecia, who was also crazy about me.

I talked to her and established somewhat of a relationship with her, but the same was true between Camille and I as well. Then, one day when I didn't walk Camille to her house after school, Lucrecia followed her while she was walking home and beat up Camille upon learning that I only wanted to be with Camille.

I was so upset with Lucrecia and with everyone who walked home with her because no one stopped the fight. Camille called me that night crying, telling me that she didn't want to be in a relationship with me anymore because I was the reason she was in a brutal fight with Lucrecia. Ever since then me and Camille stayed friends but never got back in a relationship. In fact, her mom sent her to a different middle school to get away from me.

Through all of this, I still maintained an "A" average and stayed on the honor roll. I also joined an afterschool group called Teens and Gents. We addressed issues in school and tried to come up with solutions to help our community at the time because of the gang and drug activity that plagued our city of Gary.

My closest brother, Johnny Underwood "Top Dog" died in Gary at the age of 23 and that hurt me so deeply. That same year my father died in the hospital after having surgery to fix his sleep apnea disorder. These deaths really affected me and I didn't know how to handle the negative feelings I experienced. As a result, I did whatever made me feel good to cover the hurt in my heart. I really pursued and attracted beautiful girls, I partied, shopped a lot and I started drinking alcohol. I still maintained an "A" average in school and I was on the honor roll. I was awarded most popular and best dressed before graduating Pulaski Middle School.

I went out to the skating rink in the Miller area of Gary. I got into music at that time because Hip Hop was very popular, so I joined a rap group called Le' Boys at a young age where I was a back-up Beat Box Artist to "Rock Box Arnold Turner."

I remember when the Fat Boys came to Gary; both Rock Box and I battled the Human Beat Box and we destroyed him before he got back in the limousine. Sometime after that the guys in the group got signed to Tommy Boy Records in New York.

Ray, Danny and Rock Box moved to New York while I stayed in Gary because I was too young and my mom would have never let me go to New York at the age of 15. After the group went to New York to record the album "Be For Real" I joined a local group in the Dorie Miller Projects. During that time, I met one of the best lyricists of all time, his name was Eric also known as E-Love. Shon was the second rapper, I was the beat boxer and as a group we were the best in Gary, Indiana. Our group, "The Too Def Boyz" also had our own dancers, Javon Williams and Raphael "Tweet" Brown, who later won a Grammy with the Hip Hop group, "Next" in the late 90s for best R&B group.

There used to be a big Easter talent show in Gary every year. We performed every time, rocked the crowd and always received a standing ovation. We kept a good DJ with us named Kat when we performed. He was also from Dorie Miller Projects.

Whenever we performed at the Easter talent show I would have a relationship with a girl named Punkin from the West Side of Gary. Both Punkin and I had a love for music, so backstage we would be inseparable before our performance.

We were serious about each other while we were involved in entertainment, other than that we were just good friends and stopped pursuing an intimate relationship together. In high school, I saw Regina Earvin from time to time. I remember this one particular time I noticed that she was pregnant. I was so jealous and upset to see that she was having a baby by someone other than me. Regina had a baby boy named Terry and I didn't see her after she gave birth to him. I later found out that she moved to Mississippi to live with her Grandmother and finished school there.

I joined the wrestling team at Roosevelt High School and became very good at that sport. I have always had a short and stout stature which gave me an advantage on the mat when I wrestled. I was so serious and devoted to becoming a state champion that I did not give my girlfriend any time.

I ended up breaking off my relationship with my girlfriend, Shantelle Clay. She is now the mother of Glenn Robinson III, the NBA Player. I could not spend the time with her that she deserved in the relationship with me. As a result, Shantelle started dating "Big Dog" Glenn Robinson who is also a good friend of mine.

Together they had two handsome sons named Glenn Robinson III and Gelen Robinson. During my high school years I was very focused on becoming a state champion because I had already broken the record for having the most wins in the history of Roosevelt High School wrestling. During the off season I dated a few popular females from Gary: Raychelle, Jackie, Kenya, Tomeka C., Cynthia, Tiffany, Nikki, Christina and Natalie, who later married Bernard.

I had a serious relationship with a girl named Janice for about four years. Janice loved me a lot, in fact she loved me more than I loved her and that was a problem. I was not really ready for that kind of love at my young age. My best friend, Jada would always talk to me and help me with my relationship with Janice. Jada would beg me not to hurt Janice because her love for me was real.

Janice supported my wrestling career because of her love for me. At that time, my record was 116 wins and 6 losses. I won the sectionals twice; I was regional champion, a semi state champion and "All State" Wrestler. It was so rewarding to stand at the podium to receive one of the highest medals at Mackie Square Arena in Indianapolis, Indiana.

All the while, I maintained an "A" average in school. I was voted best dressed and most popular. I was Homecoming King at Roosevelt in 1992 and I was given the Coach Holiday Award. My best friend, Jada was also an accomplished athlete at the time. She was the state champion in track & field. Jada later married Jerome who was a football player at Roosevelt. Over time, he realized that Jada and I were just best friends with each other.

Before going to college I got involved with a player from my city named Kevin. He took a liking to me because he had a lot of respect for my brother Johnny "Top Dog" who was a leader for the guys in Gary and East Chicago, Indiana. Kevin took me under his wing along with Rob and Dexter at the time and he called our group the Cleon Crew. I learned a lot about the streets from him.

At the time I didn't understand what I was getting myself into by being involved with the mob. I was just enjoying the respect others gave me because of my brother Johnny and now being involved with Kevin. While observing him, I learned that Anthony was his supplier and really we were all eating because of him. I remember one day Kevin was at his Uncle Phil's house when Phil and Stacy, his nephew got into it a scuffle.

During the scuffle Kevin accidentally got shot in the hip. I don't think Kevin's Mother ever forgave Stacy. However, Kevin never let him being shot in the hip stop him from getting money or even punishing guys who were out of line or out of pocket with him.

One day one of the guys in my neighborhood on the East Side of Gary owed me $2,500 dollars and it was taking him forever to pay me. I eventually told Kevin about the situation. He snapped and politely told me to call him and set him up to meet me because I had some product to front him to sell for me. I did exactly that and the guy met me excited as hell, but when he got in the car we surprised him and told him that we were not giving him anything to sell. In the car with Kevin driving my Delta 88, was Rayon and Rob, my partner in the Cleon Crew.

I sat in the back seat with Rob while Kevin and Rayon were in the front seat. Then they pulled over and pistol whipped him. Then Kevin drove him to a dead-end street in Gary where the beating continued. All his teeth were knocked out of his mouth and he was hit with the car. Rayon was about to kill him with Kevin's gun until I took it from him and told him it was not worth going to jail forever. After it was over, we all laughed about it and got high smoking weed.

All I could think about was, *"What am I doing? We almost killed a man over $2,500 dollars."* That's when I realized that the street life was not a game. As soon as the guy that we beat up got out of the hospital after six months he contacted me, apologized and paid me the money he owed me. It was also at that moment I realized that when you don't let people cross you in the streets, they have no choice but to respect you and also fear you at the same time. After that, my close friend that I grew up with named Corey came to have a talk with me about the incident. He told me that he was so surprised that I was involved with something like that. He told me he was going to pray for me because he thought I was losing my mind. I listened to Corey and I accepted the feedback, but I continued to live that gangster life with my guys.

That year I ended up going to the prom, I had a lot of money and respect so I stunted on that day. Kevin let me drive his BMW so I was on cloud nine. The finger waves were popular at that time, so my girl did my hair at the beauty salon called Perfections that an old "G" named Ivory owned. I went to the prom with a freshman from my school because my girlfriend Janice's parents did not want her to go. I was not mad, I just wanted to go to the prom and have fun.

The next day I returned Kevin's red BMW to him and I was happy to tell the guys about my day at the prom. When I got to Kevin's house all the guys had serious looks on their faces and books in their hands. When I walked in Rob, Kevin and Dexter all started hitting me in the head with the books they held in their hands. I was shocked and didn't understand why they were attacking me.

I eventually got tired and started fighting back, body slamming all of them one by one. Remember, I had just placed that year in the state wrestling tournament, so I was strong and fit for the battle. Once they realized that they just got body slammed they stopped attacking me. They told me they were hitting me because I had the finger waves in my head. They thought I was trying to be like the rival crew across town, Mike and his team.

As a result, they called themselves teaching me a lesson because I am a Cleon; not a peon like the rival crew. I realized then that Kevin did not like those guys at all and he did not want any of his gangsters even looking like them. My guys also recognized that I was no punk because I fought back using my wrestling skills. Some weeks later our crew had a picnic at Gleason Park to celebrate making our first million dollars as a crew.

All of Gary was there and we fed everyone out there. After hours of drinking, smoking weed and celebrating, Mike pulled up in his Corvette, jumped out the car, walked up to Dexter, hit him in the face and walked away. I guess Dexter owed Mike some money from past dealings and Mike decided to confront him at our celebration at Gleason Park.

Everyone was shocked that he would be bold enough to hit a member of our crew by himself. Kevin could not react because he was recovering from the gunshot to his hip. Rob and Dexter were too drunk so that left me. I ran to the truck to get the Mack 10 and 9mm out to retaliate. By the time I came back Mike was gone, so I started firing the Mack 10 in the air. Everyone in the park jumped in their cars and left thinking I was shooting into the crowds.

Later, Dexter resolved the issue with Mike and our crew kept moving, hustling in the streets. Our crew stepped up our game and started recruiting younger gangsters to work the operations we had set up in Glen Park. One day we got a telephone call from one of the guys and he told us that one of the fiends (drug addicts) went into his pockets and took his whole pack of rocks.

Our whole Cleon Crew went to block off the house so that none of the crack heads could leave and there was a strip search of every crack head in the house. Everybody was marched out of the house and lined up on the train tracks behind the house on their knees with their hands behind their head. They pointed a gun at their head and threatened to blow it off if they did not tell who took the dope. One of the ladies admitted to taking the dope while giving the youngster some head for a rock.

I was surprised when she told us what happened because she didn't look like a drug addict. In fact, she was a nurse at a local hospital. She took Kevin to where the dope was located, gave him some head in the bathroom and begged us not to kill her. Kevin's side chick that was extremely beautiful was with us the whole time. She knew her place because she did not say a word or get involved in the situation. She knew how to carry herself around gangsters.

We had another situation on Ridge Road. One gangster named Snasley was chasing all our guys away who were getting money on the block. Kevin decided to send me and his uncle Phil to find Snasley and warn him to stop what he was doing. On our way to the block I had a bad feeling.

I started thinking about my life and how I was raised. I was enrolled to attend college at Purdue to wrestle and I did not want to throw all that away. As a result, I had a change of heart. I convinced Phil not to go on that mission. The next day, I told Kevin we searched for Snasley the whole night, but he never came home.

That same week we went to Black Oak to serve some white boys four ounces. Kevin was recorded by the Feds talking about the sale on the phone. Dexter was on video serving the white boys and I was sitting in the passenger seat as the deal went down. Ever since then we were being followed everywhere. Kevin stayed paranoid and started snorting cocaine heavy every day. They staked out his mom's house and they even followed us to Chicago when we went to buy a real monkey to show off to people wherever we went in Gary. At that time, drug dealers in Gary were doing things like that to show off the kind of money they were playing with.

A guy named Charles had a real tiger named Sheba living in his house and the list went on and on. Kevin and I paid $5,500 for that monkey, we showed him off at the carnival in Gleason Park, took care of it for about three weeks and then for no apparent reason the monkey died in his cage.

Charles' tiger started getting too big and vicious, so he gave the animal to a friend, who subsequently donated it to the zoo. Shortly after that, the police picked up Kevin and charged him with distribution of cocaine and gave him a four-year sentence. Our whole crew was devastated by this and we all went our separate ways. Dexter got probation for his involvement and they never had enough to charge me. Rob was later killed at a Rally's drive-thru while serving a half ounce to Damon, a known killer in our city. Damon shot Rob in the head once and he died instantly. Then he shot Trent, Rob's driver six times in the face but Trent survived and Damon was later sentenced to 24 years after signing a plea. Then I went to Purdue University to wrestle and I majored in Electrical Engineering Technology. That was something my dad always wanted me to be because he was an engineer.

My best friend, Jada and my girlfriend, Janice both went to Ball State University. Jada got a scholarship like I did. She ran track and Janice majored in Nursing and Business. I did very well in the beginning of college. I made straight "A's" in all my courses and was well liked by all my teachers.

My wrestling coach, Mr. Andrews would always tell me I had the potential to be an Olympic champion, even though I took a backseat to a senior named Gabe who was an "All American." I still had the opportunity to compete my freshman year in a lot of national tournaments. My natural weight was 145 pounds, but I used to cut weight and get down to 118 pounds because I had a very muscular upper body and my legs were small. Every time I weighed in, all the coaches would come and see my actual weight for themselves. I always made weight and that scared a lot of coaches because they knew I was a dangerous wrestler.

During my stay at Purdue I became very popular as a wrestler. For some reason everyone wanted to hang around me. I met a white guy that lived in West Lafayette but didn't go to college; he was just attending a party.

He was doing cocaine with some guys, but he kept complaining about how weak the cocaine was and a light bulb went off in my head because of my connections in Gary. I knew that we were getting the best cocaine in the world that came straight off the plane in East Chicago to all the streets in Gary and Chicago.

As a result, I traveled to Gary the next day. I got about four ounces and went to the next party where I had seen Jeremy, who complained about the quality of the cocaine in West Lafayette. I gave him and his friends a sample and my whole world changed because they loved it. That city had never had cocaine that potent.

I later learned that most of the cocaine circulating in West Lafayette, Indiana was stepped on about 100 times before it reached the streets. The cocaine from Gary was only stepped on one time with B-12, so they experienced a better high than they had ever experienced in the past. Word got out about the new cocaine and it sold out immediately. In fact, I began coming to Gary and getting cocaine from my guy Sam. He was nervous about dealing with white people, so he had his right-hand man give me the dope when I came to Gary.

I made the trip so much that I had to buy from other Brick Boys like Winfred, Greedy, Chew and Danny C. At that time, I would pay about $17,500 for a brick, put another 36 ounces of B-12 on it, break it down, sell it and make about $68,000 off one brick after I turned it into two bricks. I sold each ounce for about $1,000 and it would take about four days to get rid of it all, just in Lafayette.

Then I hooked up with one of Jeremy's buddies who grew weed in West Lafayette. He would offer me 100 pounds of weed for just nine ounces of cocaine. All I did was bring the weed to Gary and started selling pounds for just $800 or $1,000 a pound depending on what the prices were in the city.

Billy was always the first person I would see when I got off the highway. He had a popular business in Gary and he knew everyone just like I did. He had a blunt spot in Dorie Miller Projects and Glen Park. All the Brick Boys like Greedy and Danny C. always got first dibs when I came to town. Billy was my main man because he would let people know the prices and how good the weed was. I would give him about three pounds at a time because he always had my money right. I would be in town for about four days and the whole 100 pounds would be gone at the fourth day.

I was always able to get back to college in time to make it to class and I still made good grades. One day Jeremy's buddy called to let me know that he was ready to trade the nine ounces for 100 pounds of weed. About the fifth time we did this I was given some weed that was green and black like tar. I did not pay it any mind, I was anxious to get to Gary and make a quick eighty thousand.

When I arrived in Gary, I gave Billy his normal. I called Greedy, Ricky and Danny C. then gave them their normal and I swear my phone started blowing up just a few hours later. People I did not know were begging me for that "Tar Weed." Even Big Mike called me trying to get that and he supplied the whole city of Gary on a regular. It sold out in two days and the people in Gary were literally hooked on that "Black Tar" weed. They gave it a name and started calling it that "Marlon."

I got back to West Lafayette, met up with my guy and asked him what was in the weed he gave me. He told me it was "Hash" and that explained why everyone loved it so much. He told me he wanted the cocaine so bad that he was afraid to tell me the truth. I told him my city went nuts over that stuff and that made me a hood celebrity.

A couple of weeks later we made a trade again but this time he gave me real marijuana (regular weed). I took it back to Gary and everyone was so hooked on that hash they did not want regular weed. It went slow and it took me about eight days to get rid of all that regular I had. I missed a whole week of school and had to really catch up when I got back.

Charles came up to my school to party with me and I introduced him to my guys including my weed connect. Somehow, he ended up exchanging numbers with my weed connect and convincing him that he could give him a better deal than I gave for the exchange. Weeks went by and I didn't hear from my weed connect, but I didn't worry because I so busy in West Lafayette. An older white guy named Doug owned a body shop in West Lafayette, so he sold all the cocaine out of his shop because my dorm was getting hot. I also had an operation going on in Brownsburg, Indiana. I was so busy with these operations that I ignored the fact that I had not heard from my weed connect. Weeks went by and then I got a call from Jeremy telling me it was urgent that I meet him in Lafayette. I very rarely went to Lafayette; instead I stayed close to campus.

I met up with Jeremy and noticed that he was high as a kite. He also looked scared. I got in the car with him and he took me to a big house out in the corn fields in the middle of nowhere. I walked inside the house into a big bedroom. My connect walked up to me with a shotgun in his hand yelling and saying that Charles and his friend took a whole load from them. He was threatening to kill me if he didn't get paid.

I did not know what was going on, but apparently, they did business with him behind my back and got robbed in the process. I looked him in his eyes and told him he was wrong for going behind my back to try to get a better deal. I called Charles, cursed him out and told him I got a shotgun at my head because of his actions and to pay those guys for the load they took. I assured them that they would either get the dope or the money for the load. However, before I was able to get them what they wanted Jeremy committed suicide and the connects' marijuana fields were burned down by the Feds. He was eventually indicted for cultivating marijuana. I was so shocked and I got very paranoid because I thought the Feds were coming for me next. I was the only guy at my dorm that had three cars and a motorcycle.

I had a Mazda RX7 hooked up with rims and tires. I had a Cadillac Deville sedan, an Expedition and a Ninja motorcycle all in the parking lot. I shut down the operation at Brownsburg. I stuck with the operation in West Lafayette. I went to Gary then returned back to school. Doug sold all the drugs at his shop. Things were strange on campus; everyone would give me a bad look everywhere.

My guy Tommy was questioned by the police and the Dean of Students. As a result, he was kicked out of college. I was interviewed by the Dean of Students and was told that my name was being plastered all around campus as the campus drug lord. Then Coach Andrews, my wrestling coach had a long talk with me about how I was going down the wrong path. I didn't get kicked out of school, but the police came to my dorm, searched it and found $170,000 in a duffle bag. I was able to get it back because Doug who owned the body shop claimed the money. He had the business and the taxes to prove that it was his money. They raided Tommy's room and found crack. Tommy ended up getting time for possession of cocaine and was sentenced to about four years.

Doug got the money back and I packed up all my things. I dropped out of college after my second year. I had a 3.8 grade point average and a promising wrestling career. I left it all behind and moved back to Gary. I kept the business arrangement with Doug. I just had to leave the campus because eventually I would have been indicted. My girlfriend at the time, Janice, wanted to be close to me so she dropped out of college and moved in with her parents in Gary.

Once I made it back to Gary, I formed my own crew with Marvin, Charlie and the Jones Brothers. I paid Marvin to drive to West Lafayette once a week to drop off work at Doug's body shop. He was happy because he needed the money to take care of his nine kids. Most of my money and profits came from Doug. I made ok money in Gary with my crew. I really hustled there to make sure my guys could eat because it was hard at that time to get in the game. If you were not plugged into work with someone or if you had no money you were on the outside looking in; watching the players make all the money and finesse all the girls. I was plugged in and had the money, so I made sure my people were eating. After about eight months I went back to a big college party the AKA's were throwing and everyone treated me like a celebrity.

I mean everyone was excited to see me and they missed my association on campus. I was approached by an Asian girl who looked just like Halle Berry, but she had Chinese eyes. This girl introduced herself to me, told me that she heard about me and that she needed help. I asked her what's up and she made a proposition to me. She said she would have sex with me for one week straight every day if I helped her get her mom a heart pacemaker.

After she stated her request, she immediately started crying and dropped down to my feet begging me to have sex with her. This girl shocked the hell out of me; I could not believe she was coming at me like this. I brought her to her feet and asked her how much she needed to help her mom. She told me she needed $3,500. I had ten thousand dollars in my pocket. I counted out five thousand dollars, gave it to her and told her to help her mom. She took my phone number and left. I also told her I did not want any sex from her. I really could not party that hard at the AKA joint because I could not believe that happened, so I just chilled out drinking my Grey Goose vodka. I stayed the night at Doug's mansion and went back to Gary the next morning.

Since I had been back in Gary I noticed that the city was on fire, everybody was getting high either on weed, crack or alcohol. There was a crack house on every block. Nurses, doctors, firemen, teachers, mothers and fathers were all getting high. On the flip side there were a lot of kingpins in Gary, every one of them was making millions driving Mercedes, Cadillac's, BMWs, Corvettes, trucks, etc.

All of us who had the streets were young and rich having fun, shopping, taking trips, having a lot of sex and spending money all through Gary at all the clubs. I remember after Sam ordered a shipment, he had Charlie pick it up and bring it to him. Charlie brought it to me to show me before he took it to Sam. Charlie popped the trunk and there were about 15 bricks all with stamps of a scorpion on it. I could not believe my eyes. I learned that he bought it from Mike who was our rival before I went to college. Mike was the man to get the bricks from, along with Thomas, Bobby, Charles, Chocolate, Sam, Winfred, Greedy and Ant. Stacy was locked up and Mike's brother Darnell died in a motorcycle accident. I, on the other hand continued my dealings in Lafayette and I kept my crew eating real good in Gary.

I eventually broke up with Janice because she was just too much of a good girl, I was a player and I got tired of hurting her. I hooked up with Keisha, who had two boys. First we lived in Concord on the West Side of Gary where all the vice lords were and I kept a low profile because I was one of the guys in their hood. I eventually bought a townhouse in Highland, Indiana for my new family and Keisha was so happy for the life I provided for her.

I bought her a new car, jewelry and took care of her two boys. I had $450,000 so I was able to make sure that we did not want for anything. Every time I took my cars out to drive around in Gary people acted like they were watching a parade when they saw me.

I took the time out to help Keisha's mom get into rehab and paid for it. I also took the time out to find Keisha's biological father, whom she had never met. We learned that his last name was Flowers and he had died a long time ago. Keisha met all her aunts and cousins on that side.

She also learned that he fathered a son with a girl from Dorie Miller, a year before Keisha was born. That son turned out to be my childhood friend Kenneth, whom I had known since I was five years old. I talked to Kenneth and he confirmed, via what his grandmother had told him, that his biological father's last name was Flowers. Then I told him about Keisha, my girlfriend. They went to the same high school together but never talked to each other.

After living like a king for many years all hell broke loose. Joe got caught going to Minnesota with twenty bricks and from that point a big investigation was brought about in Gary, Indiana in regards to the drug activity that had been going on there.

As a result of the investigation, the Feds picked up all the Brick Boys in Gary and charged them all with conspiracy. That drug bust shocked the community and everybody was scared to do anything.

One guy I had never seen before came over to where my crew hung out, claiming he was from Memphis and he wanted to buy nine ounces and showed me that he had all the money. I took his phone number and told him I would call him. I thought about it because I had a bad feeling about him so I decided not to make the sale with him. I'm glad I didn't because I later found out that he was working with the Feds. That same guy got the work from a guy named Big Vic and he ended up catching a charge over that.

During that time while the streets were on edge I started having problems with my guy Doug that owned the body shop. Doug lost a hundred pounds because he got seriously strung out on cocaine. He started being short on the money he owed me and coming up with bogus excuses. He would write me checks for thirty thousand and it would bounce on my bank account. He eventually closed the body shop because he had lost control. I had to cut all ties with him still owing me $120,000.

I was so upset with him because he used to be a solid, trustworthy person and he changed for the worse. I had no one I could trust that could take his spot, so I had to take over the operation myself. I did not do that long because I got pulled over by a state trooper on the highway and he called about eight other troopers to the scene and they searched my Cadillac from top to bottom. I did not have any drugs, but I had about $30,000 in a hidden compartment that I had built in my car. They took me to jail and took my car to search again. They could only hold me for a limited time without a charge so they eventually let me go. Charlie came and picked me up from the station and we went to get my Cadillac out of the pound. My car was torn to pieces, but my money was never found.

Charlie told me then that he was moving out of town because he was spooked about the Feds busting our guys. He told me that he had ten bricks and about $70,000, which he planned to use to get on in Atlanta. He gave me a hug and I have not seen him since that time. I also told myself that my operation in West Lafayette was over and I never went back. I laid low and stayed in the house with my girlfriend Keisha for months. My whole crew broke up and I was the only one left in Gary wondering what was about to happen to me.

As time went on I started to realize that I was safe. I stopped selling drugs because I had no connect and I got a job working at LeeMar Steel Corporation in East Chicago, Indiana. They were paying me about $500 a week. It felt good not selling drugs because I did not have the stress that came with that lifestyle. I was living a normal life for about five years until me and Keisha began having problems. The money was dwindling down and it scared Keisha because she was used to such a lavish lifestyle with me and it all started to change. Keisha and I broke up so she moved to Indianapolis and left me in the house by myself. At that point I had reached my bottom.

I dropped out of college, I lost my girlfriend, I had a job paying pennies compared to what I was used to and I ran out of money. I had a long talk with my oldest brother Charlie. He always had game ready for me in my life. I learned so much about women, money and life from him. Then I went to my mom's house like a baby and laid in the bed with her, with my arms wrapped around her waist crying the whole night. The next morning, I heard her reading the Bible; it woke me up because when my mom reads God's word you can feel the Holy Spirit.

My hairs rose up on my body, I connected to the universe and everything was clear to me. I knew I had to surrender my life to God. I attended the meeting at my old Kingdom Hall and everyone was excited to see me. They called me the Prodigal Son coming home and they welcomed me back with open arms.

I talked to my childhood friend Kenneth and he was happy to see me back with Jehovah. We also talked about his half-sister and he told me he thought about finding his biological family and having a relationship with them, but he told me that his stepfather, Earl was his father and he was going to end it with that. After attending the meetings for a while I progressed very fast.

The brothers used me a lot to help out in the congregation and I always took pride in my assignments. I started Pioneering and attended Pioneer school. It was there that I learned the art of reaching people, showing personal interest in others, using illustrations and vivid hyperbole when teaching others.

I became an excellent Teacher and Public Speaker. I also developed the art of listening to others, using eye contact and good body language when communicating. I went to Bethel, New York to work. While I was there, I dated a few spiritual sisters.

I got serious with one of them, her name was Nikki. However, she was not willing to move back to Gary, Indiana with me so we ended the relationship. After coming back to Gary and getting settled in my congregation again I was appointed as a Ministerial Servant. My job was to teach and assist the Elders at my hall. As a Ministerial Servant I had a lot of work on my plate. I did a lot of teaching from the Bible at different congregations in Gary. Word spread around that I was an excellent Teacher and I got invited to give talks in Chicago, Michigan, New York and throughout Indiana Kingdom Halls. I later met the Artist formerly known as Prince at a Kingdom Hall and we talked quite a bit.

I told him about my life coming back to the truth and he told me how he studied with Larry Graham and was baptized. I was happy to see someone like Prince serving Jehovah. I was confident that I was in the right place. I later met a young Sister in Michigan named Vatina who went to the Kingdom Hall; we dated for a short time and then got married. Vatina is a good person who was humble and we just connected spiritually and always got along. Vatina got my attention because she had long hair down to her buttocks and her father was 70% Cherokee Indian.

I got to admit, Vatina and I had a great life together. One day while we were at home we met with a guy named Brian who sold insurance for American Income Life and he was trying to sell us insurance. Brian and I talked for hours and he forgot why he came to my house because he was very intrigued with me. He then asked me if I was interested in the insurance business and he told me based on our conversation he thought I could be extraordinarily successful. I asked him what kind of money could I make and he told me that I could make millions. He showed me his last week's paycheck where he made ten thousand dollars in one week.

After I saw that check I asked him what I needed to do to make that kind of money. He instructed me on how I could get my license and within one month I had my life license to sell insurance in the state of Indiana. During my training with American Income Life, I learned that this company had a niche market with all the unions in the United States and New Zealand. This company provided insurance for all union members because most union members lose their insurance upon retirement so American Income Life was available to provide permanent insurance for the rest of their lives.

I found this to be an easy sale for me because of my background in public speaking, Pioneer school and college. I learned that if I was able to paint a picture to the client, helping them to see the need and the urgency to buy insurance, I would sell a lot of it. My first week with American Income Life I had twenty appointments. Out of the twenty appointments, I sold eighteen. I made over 10,000 dollars in seven days. That impressed my managers Bob and Scott. Scott used to be a college basketball coach and Bob was an ex-football player. Scott worshipped me, and told me that he had never met anyone like me.

He told me I had a million dollar smile and an awesome personality that people couldn't say no to. The things Scott told me reminded me of school days and how I was well loved by my teachers and the students. After my first month with the company I broke the production record for the month, 51 thousand and they featured me in the company Spotlight magazine talking about my accomplishments in such a short time. They had my picture and a whole page article discussing the record I broke in such a short time. That record had been held for ten years before I started working for the company. I came along and shattered it to pieces.

In a few months I was promoted to General Agent. Then after making 250 thousand I was promoted again to Master General Agent. I was promoted to this level based on my own personal production even though this was a manager contract. I later got my own office and started recruiting agents to work under me with American Income Life. I worked in the morning recruiting and doing interviews. Then I sold insurance later that evening. The only days I did not go out into the field was my meeting days at the Kingdom Hall. Eventually I had 40 agents working under me at my office in Hammond, Indiana. Every month my agency produced over $120,000 a month in production and over a million dollars a year. Out of that money, Bob and Scott took about $40,000 each, per month from my agency.

That means they took home $40,000 dollars each, just off my office in Hammond. However, they had ten other Master General Agents bringing in revenue as well. They were millionaires, especially Scott because he was a State General Agent. Bob was an RGA under Scott and I was under Bob. In 2002, I broke the company record with American Income Life for writing the most business in a year. Since the existence of American Income Life no one has written more business than me.

I was very proud of myself and I got a lot of recognition for breaking so many company records. They hired a company to come and record a documentary of my life showing how an African-American from Gary, Indiana was surviving the streets and having major success in corporate America as a Master General Agent Insurance Salesman. I also broke another record for writing the most business as a manager. My agency out wrote all of the other agencies under Scott. I proved to be successful as an individual agent and as a manager.

The company had a magazine called the "Spotlight" and I made the cover of the magazine. I was so amazed and proud to see my face on the cover of a magazine that was distributed worldwide. In all 50 states, millions of people saw the magazine and I became a household name in the insurance business from that point forward. I was asked by the company to put an example presentation together on how I closed the clients. After I did that, they copied the presentation, mass produced it and sent it to every agency in the United States under American Income Life. Many State General Agents invited me to come and give seminars on this art of sales that I created.

I traveled throughout the U.S. giving the same speech on the skills and knowledge needed to achieve such success. I took all the knowledge I learned as a child growing up as a Jehovah's Witness and everything I learned after that and developed a system on how anyone can be successful in insurance sales if only they follow my system using the 48 laws of being successful in sales. The laws I follow actually work. Just like there are laws of gravity, laws of attraction, and laws of love; there are also laws of being successful in sales.

Later that year the company had a convention designed to honor all the success and accomplishments of American Income Life. The company flew my family to see me be honored. Angel, Tina, Melody and my wife were there but my mom Virginia was scared to fly so she did not come, but she was there in spirit. The company set us all up at a 5 star hotel in Orlando, Florida. My whole family had suites and was treated with the utmost respect. We had limousine service, VIP treatment and sat at the front of the stage at the event. This was the classiest event I had ever attended. Everyone was dressed up in tuxedos or elegant dresses.

There were a few celebrities there supporting the company and there were about 2,000 agents along with their spouses and family that attended. The only agents that attended were the ones that qualified to be there. The awards banquet started out with a lavish three course meal and then there was a real Phantom of the Opera show presented. A few award winning authors gave presentations. Scott spoke, Roger gave a talk and they presented awards in many categories: SGA Awards, MGA Awards, RGA Awards, GA Awards, SA Awards and then the Agents. Scott, my State General Agent received the SGA Award along with a few others. Bob received the RGA Award. I received the MGA Award along with many others. They saved the best award for last which was the Record Breaking Annual Lead Premium Award. I was presented the award by Roger and Scott.

They gave me a bonus on stage for $50,000 dollars. It was a big check that I held up to the whole crowd and everyone gave me a standing ovation. In my speech I thanked everyone involved in my road to success. I also encouraged all the Sales Agents to learn to be like water. Water can flow, water can crash, water can turn into ice; water can adjust and conform to anything.

If we learn to become all things to all people, we will win their favor and they will buy whatever you tell them to buy because you related to them and they trust in your service. 80% of the sale, the client buys into you; the other 20% of the sale is the product you are selling. So, if you work on yourself applying the laws of attraction and the laws of sales, you will, without a doubt achieve success. Afterwards, I shook so many hands and signed so many autographs for the Agents and their families that came to the awards banquet. Later my whole family that came to Florida with me went to Disney World together and had so much fun.

The next day we flew back to Indiana to rest. During that time my wife was pregnant and within a few weeks she gave birth to my daughter, Mahiah.

Mahiah was 10 pounds at birth. She was a big baby with curly hair and so lovable. From birth, Mahiah was attached to me. We have a special bond with each other that words can't describe. Every day after work she would hear the doorbell and run to jump into my arms. Mahiah loved when I came home with barbecue, she loved the taste of the sauce in her mouth and would get so excited to eat it. I loved the look in her eyes of adoration towards me. My schedule included going to meetings three days a week, I worked six days out of the week, I was very busy and my relationship with my wife became estranged.

At the Kingdom Hall, the brothers appointed me as an Elder in the Christian congregation. I became even busier counseling the brothers, teaching at book study and meetings, as well as preaching in the community. At the same time, I continued to have success with my insurance business. The following year I achieved my goals of being the #1 Agent and the #1 MGA again. The company convention was held in the Bahamas and all the agents that qualified stayed at the Atlantis. Once again, we stayed in a suite and it was great. I was able to mingle with all the agents across the United States.

Everyone took their turn talking to me about the insurance business and how they can improve the sales in their business. The convention started with a three course meal, followed by entertainment. The awards banquet was similar to the convention in Florida. I received the same awards that I got the year before, Agent of the Year and the Master General Agent Award. I did not get a bonus because I did not break my own record. The association afterwards was very positive, my wife and I left the hotel and traveled on foot to the village in the area.

There were people selling Jamaican dishes and it smelled very good, so we stopped at a little restaurant and bought a few dishes to taste. While at the restaurant a little lady walked up to me looking possessed (psychic) and told me I was the wrong "color." I asked her what she meant by that and she told me that the company I did business with wanted me to be the SGA (State General Agent) of Chicago but I was the wrong color. She said they would give the position to someone who was envious of me and she said that I needed to be careful. I brushed her off as though she was crazy and went on my way back to the hotel.

After returning home back to business as usual I continued my success with the company. I developed business relationships with union figures like Jimmy Hoffa, Jr. and Jules Pagano. Jimmy Hoffa, Jr. gave me a miniature truck with his signature as memorabilia for my office. I showed everyone I interviewed to show the close relationship between American Income Life and the unions like the Teamsters. The company made Scott, my State General Agent at the time, the Vice President of the company and his team made Bob the State General Agent of Chicago, whom I was under.

Immediately, I remembered what the psychic lady told me in the Bahamas about being the wrong color and I got chills down my spine. Every one of the agents in the company was very confident that I would be State General Agent of Chicago but that did not happen. I never believed in psychics, but how did this woman know this was about to happen and she had never met me before? That woman was right when she said that they wanted me to have the position but I'm just the wrong color because Roger flew me to Waco, Texas to talk to me and had that look on his face that he was sorry. He explained that I may become SGA over Indiana or Michigan in the future and he encouraged me to keep working hard being the best.

I was happy about our meeting, but I always kept in mind what that psychic told me at the Atlantis, in the Bahamas. As a result, I kept my mind focused on being SGA in Indiana or Michigan one day. While having continued success in the insurance business, I kept progressing spiritually in the organization. I was given the privilege to instruct at the circuit assembly held in Romeoville, Illinois. There were about 3,000 Witnesses there attending the meeting and everyone enjoyed the part I gave. My mom was so proud of me; she told me that I was her pride and joy in life.

I took that to heart and cherished how she felt about me. In my city a lot of my childhood friends heard about my success and the change I made in my life. As a result, many of them got into the insurance business and some of them became Jehovah's Witnesses. I was well respected because people knew where I came from and to see my life progress, made them respect me more.

I had one strange encounter during field service where we would go out in the city of Gary, Indiana preaching about God's kingdom and what it would do for mankind. During service in the housing projects, I knocked on a door; lo and behold it was the guy that we almost beat to death years ago.

We both stared at each other for about five minutes. I almost walked away, but the Spirit of God came over me and I began telling him about the Kingdom of God and that I had changed my life to serve Jehovah. I told him that the whole world is being influenced by the devil and we must follow the Bible's principles if we want to have a happy life.

After listening to me he started crying and said he was happy for me and that he too wanted to find happiness for himself. I started a Bible study with him and after nine months he got baptized as one of Jehovah's Witnesses serving Jehovah.

He started going to the meetings and preaching door-to-door about the kingdom. This experience with him showed me how God works and that He is truly the one who causes things to be.

In the meantime, I still had the insurance game on lock in Indiana and Chicago but I still had not been appointed SGA yet. One day, out of the clear blue sky, my RGA Bob started having problems. He would call me every day checking on the amount of production my agency was producing. I was already the top MGA in Chicago, producing more than all the other MGA's and all of a sudden it was never enough for Bob.

I could not believe he had the nerve to treat me like that after I made millions for his organization. I thought about the psychic and what she said in the Bahamas. I don't believe in psychics, but that lady was absolutely correct with what she told me. I continued to get pressured daily to produce more and more. I eventually got tired and resigned. Roger and Scott, the CEO and Vice President called me every day. I never answered even though I truly loved them both for the opportunity they gave me. It really hurt to avoid their phone calls.

I focused all my attention on my little daughter Mahiah, whom I love. I had seven digits in the bank so I had the money to take care of my family unemployed for about a month. Soon as I decided to look to broker an insurance contract, every insurance company after finding out who I was and after looking at my financials and production history, offered me the highest contract to receive in the business. I was offered 150% contracts, 130% contracts and 120% contracts from five different companies. The contracts I was offered were higher than the SGA contract with American Income Life and mainly the contract I have with the company which was 70%. With a 70% contract I was making about $850,000 a year, so just imagine what I could have made with a 150% contract or a 130% contract.

I opened American Freedom Financial LLC and began getting contracted with all five companies. Those companies treated me like a king. I mean they gave me whatever I wanted. I moved into a big office in Highland, Indiana. I hired a secretary, started interviewing in the morning and running appointments selling insurance in the evening. The first month my company made $200,000 dollars.

I felt like I was in a dream because I was making so much money. In six months I had thirty agents out in the field contracted with American Freedom Financial, "My Company." By the end of the year I had 100 agents contracted all across the United States. I created a standard presentation for all the agents to use in the field. I even created a video and sent it out to all agents to view and learn my art of sales using "The 48 Laws of Sales" that I created. As a result, American Freedom Financial produced $2.4 million in annual Lead Premiums. I had a great niche market and I did my own mailings from my office. I had a team putting the mailings together and sending them off daily. My niche market included postal workers, seniors, new homebuyers and individuals that made over $200,000 a year.

When the leads came back I sent the leads to the agent who resided at that city and state. Since my company provided the leads for all the agents I had all my managers at a 70% contract and they gave the agents they managed a 50% contract. My company, American Freedom Financial LLC made the other 80% or 60% depending on which company the Agents used.

Business was great; we had a 70% closing ratio as a company and an 80% persistency ratio. I was happy because it showed that the agents were paying attention to what I was teaching them in the video. They understood the art of sales and "The 48 Laws of Sales" that I discovered through the process of selling insurance.

I had a flashback from the past while at home watching TV and my phone rang. The person on the phone with a voice I could never forget asked to speak to Vashonna. I paused and said, "Regina is this you?" She said, "Is this Marlon Underwood?" I said, "Yes." Then she told me that she must have dialed the wrong number because her friend Vashonna had a number similar to mine.

We were very happy to hear from each other. We talked about the old school days. Both of us kept talking about, "What's the chance of this happening?" We even laughed about the encounter.

When we got off the telephone, after an hour of talking, I felt chills down my back and arms from thinking about how much I really wanted a relationship with her the very first time I saw her. Being married at the time, I knew that would never happen so I got back to my regular schedule in life. It was nice to talk to Regina again and I thought about her for days after that.

A year later I was waiting in the barbershop for a haircut. Then Regina came inside, looked at me with a smile and said, "Marlon, look at you with your chubby self." I just laughed and told her I had been eating and working and I didn't work out like I did when I wrestled. Once again, we talked for a while because we were happy to see each other. She told me that she was running an internet business called "Good Scents Oils." She had been selling oils and sugar scrubs for 18 years. I told her about what I had been doing and Regina was so happy for me.

I told her that I thought if she worked insurance part time she would be successful because of her personality and her experiences with her internet business. I told her to meet me in my office in Highland so we could talk about it further. After our meeting Regina decided to give it a try.

She went out and got her insurance license, we both would go and run appointments together while I trained her. She caught on very quickly, wrote a lot of business and made a lot of money. Regina impressed me so much as a businesswoman, when she wrote 10,000 dollars in one day. At the same time, we became close friends and our relationship was getting stronger and stronger.

One day in my office while doing paperwork; we looked at each other and smiled. Then we kissed passionately for a long time. In that moment I realized that I was falling in love with Regina.

Later that night I went to our congregation meeting with my wife and daughter. However, everything was a blur because I could not believe that I could love a woman other than my wife. I felt as though I had betrayed my family, especially my daughter Mahiah. I also became unfaithful to my God Jehovah, by allowing myself to love another woman. I fought against it for a while but lost the battle every time.

I began to get depressed, so I started getting materialistic and buying things to make myself feel better. I bought a 750 BMW, a Hummer and a 1974 Cadillac Eldorado. I also went on elaborate shopping sprees almost every week.

Regina realized that she was neglecting her "Good Scents Oils" business and she wanted to open a shop in Gary, Indiana so I agreed to invest in both Billy and Regina's business together. I gave Billy $20K for a down payment for the building on Broadway and invested in "Good Scents Oils" so she could have her business in the same building networking with the barbershop.

All three of us grew up together and we were happy we had all been able to do something positive in the city of Gary. Billy did pay me back the money I loaned to him, but he was not happy to see me and Regina together in a relationship, so the relationship between me and Billy became estranged.

So, not only were Regina and I in love with one another we were also business partners. I was very proud of myself and at the same I was torn because I had a family at home. Eventually the truth came out, I was seen at a restaurant with Regina and they observed Regina feeding me. The person called my wife and told her. One day while at Regina's home my phone accidentally called my wife while I was telling Regina I loved her. Vatina reported the issues with me to the Elders at my congregation.

They gave me some counsel, but afterwards I was so embarrassed and humiliated by my conduct that I stepped down as an Elder and I stopped going to the Kingdom Hall. Vatina knew in her heart that I was in love with Regina so she left me in a $600,000 house to myself and took my daughter Mahiah with her. I became more depressed, so I started drinking more and staying out late at the bars.

Regina really felt bad for me because she knew how much I loved my daughter, but she was torn, just like I was torn. I got over it and every week or every two weeks I traveled to spend time with Mahiah. Sometimes I would bring her back to Indiana and spend time with her there. Through the whole process I kept my relationship with my daughter. Vatina and I became very good friends. I later got divorced and I moved in with Regina while my house stayed empty and I paid the bills there. I also found out that when I first fell in love with Regina, she was married to a kingpin out of Chicago who was in the Feds. We were both married to someone else at the time.

Since my relationship became damaged with God and I had extra time on my hand I went back into my past and rekindled my love for music.

I hooked up with an old partner in music named "Tension." I incorporated my own entertainment company, named it "My Life Entertainment" and signed him to my label. By this time, Charlie came back from Atlanta after running off with all those bricks and began helping me with the label. The contract that Tension had with My Life Entertainment was a 360 contract.

That is always a good contract to have on an Artist that you plan on investing a lot of money in because you can ensure that you will get your investment back quicker. After my deal signing with Tension, he immediately started working in the studio with a Producer named "Dead Bodies." Tension wrote a hit song in our city called "Birds Chirpin" along with many others. I executive produced a song with hip hop underground king Bun-B that Tension and Dean put together called "Dem Po Po's." We featured IVO The Grand Duke on Tension's mix tape as well as Scarfo and Tex songs like "Scary Gary" and "Feels Like Home." The mix tape was a hit in our city and we end up circulating 10K CD's throughout Gary and Indianapolis. A few months later, we did a concert in Indianapolis at the Conseco Fieldhouse. We were selling CD's and T-shirts outside the venue.

My Hummer at the time was stationed outside with all of Tension's marketing materials plastered on the vehicle. I also brought my 750 BMW down for the look. Also performing were Shawnna, Ludacris, Bun-B and others. Tension and another Artist named Hit performed first. Tension started performing "Birds Chirpin" and everyone in the Fieldhouse went crazy. There were over ten thousand people at the concert.

While Tension performed I had the chance to pass out "Birds Chirpin" Volume One to the crowd from the stage. After Tension's performance we hooked up with Bun-B and blew a couple blunts, talked and left out when it was time for Bun-B to perform. By the time Bun-B performed the crowd was really hyped and was going crazy. The only thing that was missing was Pimp–C and you were able to recognize his presence being missed throughout the performance.

Everyone who had lighters put it in the air for Pimp-C, rest in peace. Shawnna and Ludacris got on stage and snapped with their performance, leaving the crowd yelling at the top of their voices. The whole crowd was smoking and passing blunts around.

Regina and I were happy to see Tension making a name for himself representing "My Life Entertainment." After getting back home, Tension returned to the studio and while he did that I hooked up with the promoter named Mic-Check. We both began promoting shows throughout Gary, Merrillville and Chicago. Both of us promoted shows with Glenn Jones, Chico DeBarge, Miki Howard and many others.

Miki Howard and I developed a personal relationship after learning we both grew up as Jehovah's Witnesses. We stayed in contact and communicated years afterwards.

In the meantime, Tension wrote a hit song in our city called, "Mammay Doe" which means it's "official." After seeing the reaction from the city, I knew if I could put money behind it eventually it would go platinum.

As a result, I went straight to Radio. I had a meeting in Chicago with all the DJ's including DJ Ferris and made arrangements for the song to be played on the regular. Once I saw the reaction from Chicago and Gary, then I went to a radio guy in Memphis who was associated with Yo Gotti and hired him to work the song throughout the United States. I went through a lot of cash, but it was worth it because the song hit in the Top Five charts for about six months.

Tension began doing interviews everywhere including Chicago, Birmingham and a few other locations. My company, "My Life Entertainment" had Tension doing shows everywhere. Some of the shows were recorded and you can see them online now. There are videos on worldstarhiphop.com or you can see the videos on You Tube by typing Tension or My Life Entertainment in the search box.

While Tension was busy getting famous, My Life Entertainment embarked on a new project promoting "Basketball Wives." I signed contracts with the Executive Producer, Shaunie O'Neal to do shows in different cities promoting them and boosting ratings for the show.

While all these things were taking place Regina and I were traveling all over the world to places like Europe. We visited all the ancient castles in Europe and then we went to Amsterdam. While I was there, I smoked some of the best Cush in the world. While visiting Cancun, Mexico we had a lot of fun going horseback riding and eating at the finest restaurants.

The last time I was in Mexico I was with my ex-wife Vatina and we won a dance contest while she was pregnant with Mahiah. We also spent time in Puerto Vallarta, Mexico shopping and enjoying life. One of the last countries that we visited was Argentina.

My agency won that trip from one of the insurance companies we wrote for and Argentina was a very unique, beautiful place to visit. It was where I saw my first polo game, live and up close.

Back in the States, I did an all-white party for Shaunie O'Neal. Tension and Will from Day 26 performed at the party. A few NBA stars attended the party to show their support. I had a lot of fun promoting the Basketball Wives, people always came to support it and at the same time the fans were able to meet them personally at the events.

During the process, I developed a personal relationship with Shaunie O'Neal.

Shaunie liked being in Chicago, eating at nice restaurants while being escorted in a stretch limo, staying in the best hotels and of course eating Garrett's popcorn, which she loved. I used to have to make special trips to get that for her. In fact, you can see a few of my shows with Shaunie on You Tube and World Star Hip Hop. If you type in "My Life Entertainment" or "Shaunie O'Neal and Tension" you will see how successful those events were.

While promoting the shows I got a call from an Executive at BET who wanted my Artist, Tension to compete in a rap contest on 106 & Park. I paid a hefty cost, but it was worth it because Tension would be getting more exposure.

Tension already had a song on the radio that was playing throughout the U.S. "Mammay Doe." If you look on You Tube or World Star you can see the video made for the song. That video is one of the best videos made in Gary, Indiana. I had my new Bentley Arnage in the video and the whole city supported us while it was being made. There were also a few Artists from Chicago who came and supported us. The whole city was behind us and could not wait for Tension to compete on 106 & Park, representing Gary. I hooked up with an older promoter named Prime Time, who managed a dance group called Kruciial Kreatiionz.

We decided to allow them to be the dancers behind Tension on stage. As a result, I flew Tension, the dancers, Prime Time and JTP Productions to New York. JTP Productions was made up of three people: Lil Man (Aurelio Kidd) the CEO, J Trax (Engineer) and Yoson Tala. My Life Entertainment collaborated with JTP so that the only thing we needed after that was a distribution deal. I had my own in-house Engineer, Beat Maker, Writer and Rapper. I also had my own radio guy who made sure that radio would play my music.

Once in New York, we made sure everyone was situated and a few hours later Tension had to be at 106 & Park for rehearsal. After rehearsal we had about three hours until the show began. Everyone was excited backstage; I believe this was the first time anyone from Gary appeared on 106 & Park. In the beginning, Rocsi and Terrence, the Hosts for 106 & Park introduced themselves to me and wished us good luck. In the building where 106 & Park was held I noticed that there were other shows going on, Kimora Lee Simmons, Russell Simmons' wife was there. She was scheduled to appear at a show in the building, so we took pictures with her before Tension performed.

Tension eventually took the stage and had the crowd going. We had people in the audience with Mammay Doe shirts "Yelling Mammay!" People across the United States were familiar with the song because it was played on the radio daily. There were two other acts that performed after Tension.

Once the votes came in Rocsi read off the winner and of course it was Tension. His performance from 106 & Park can be seen on YouTube right now. After leaving the building we took a stretched limo and partied all night celebrating the victory.

Tension cried for hours because he was so happy he won 106 & Park and the world witnessed it. "My Life Entertainment" had made a statement in Hip Hop without a record deal. I realized at that moment, we were closer to getting a deal signed.

Back home the city was celebrating, the radio stations were promoting the victory we had and everyone was happy. While "Mammay Doe" was blowing up in the streets, My Life Entertainment worked out an agreement with World Star Hip Hop. As a result, I found the best Strippers and Dancers across America, got them on contract and had them do exotic videos. Then I gave the videos to the owner "Q" to put them on World Star.

This was a success because once the videos were up on World Star, promoters from everywhere called me to book the Dancer to do a show at their club. The price ranged from $1,000-$2,500 to book the girl to do a show depending on the popularity of the Dancer.

"My Life Entertainment" was also paid by World Star Hip Hop to put the video on the site ranging from $1,500 to $2,500 each video. The only problem me and "Q" had was that he didn't want my logo on the video advertising my entertainment company.

After doing business for a while he didn't complain when I had the "My Life Entertainment" logo put on some videos. I developed a personal relationship with one of the dancers named "Platinum Dior" who was being booked across the States at least twice a week.

One time we did a show in North Carolina and South Carolina back to back. During her stage show she had all the Ballers come out and she made ten thousand dollars on stage dancing. The same thing happened in Houston, Texas; Platinum made a lot of money on stage. I believe that video is on You Tube right now, I remember seeing it under another promotion company in Houston. I traveled with Platinum doing a lot of shows, to the point where I was never home.

I eventually got a call from Mic-Check telling me that the "Meet the Browns" cast would be in Chicago. Since they would already be close we could book them to do a show at the Genesis Center in Gary for $15,000. I agreed to do the show, signed the contract and paid the fifteen grand. This was special because everyone loved the show especially the Mann's couple and I knew the city would support it. We got all the churches in the city involved including Chicago and promoted everywhere.

The cost to attend was $40 per person and I believe about 2,500 people showed up. The show was a success. The Mann's couple did their skits and warmed the heart of everyone who attended. The Mayor of our city, Rudy Clay was there. He came to the stage after the show and gave us the keys to the city. Me and Regina had a good time because we were able to spend time together, normally I would be on the road.

Next, Tension was asked to perform at Adrianna's and we made a big statement. Shawnna, the rapper who was signed to Ludacris DTP was also there. That day I bought the bar and threw ten thousand dollars at the crowd while Tension performed. By that time, I noticed the crowd singing along with Tension as he performed.

Afterwards, Shawnna and my whole crew wanted to go get breakfast, but I declined and told Shawnna we would get together later. My guy Lil Man talked to Shawnna on the phone and made arrangements for us to come to her house. I sent my Stepson Terry to go with Lil Man and when they got there Shawnna was kind of upset that I didn't come.

Terry made it clear at the house that I was in love with his mother and that nothing was going to happen between me and Shawnna. They laughed it off, had a good time eating and drinking, then they went back to Gary.

A few weeks later I called Shawnna and asked her to do a song with my Artist Tension since we were all from the same area. Tension laid down his verse on the track and then my Producer J Trax sent the track to Shawnna to put her verse to it. While waiting on the music to get finished I got a call to come to Shawnna's video shoot and they wanted me to bring the Bentley to put in the video. Shawnna had a Lambo, so with both cars we made a good look for her video.

I went to my house to get ready. I saw that my girl Regina was looking kind of upset because I had been working a lot and not spending time with her. I got the Bentley cleaned up and I put on at least $180,000 worth of jewelry. I threw on my Gucci shirt, belt, shoes and I was fresh to death. The minute I told my girl I was making an appearance in Shawnna's video Regina snapped, she snatched off all my jewelry and ripped off my shirt. I realized how strong Regina was in that moment.

After breaking free from her I ran outside and jumped in the Bentley. Then I drove straight to my jeweler to get my chains fixed. There I was scratched up and breathing hard and all I wanted to do was fix my jewelry. I knew I had a problem with materialism, but I ignored it. I later called Shawnna's Management and told them I was not able to make the video shoot.

I felt bad about that because relationships are important in the entertainment business and I felt like I let Shawnna down. Regina eventually called to apologize and I told her I knew that I hadn't been spending time with her, so I spent the whole night making love to her until she was satisfied. To this day I never released the song Tension made with Shawnna and I never talked on the phone with her again. In fact, Shawnna has the masters in her possession since she was the last person to lay her verse to the track.

One day after seeing an insurance client in Gary I saw a young lady walking up to a brick house. I noticed that she was very attractive, and I felt at the moment, that she would be a good candidate (model) to promote on World Star. I pulled up in my 750 BMW at the time and asked her name and she told me D.D. (Darlisa). I explained to her what I did and asked her if she was interested.

She told me that her boyfriend was just murdered, her kids didn't have a father and that was her main concern at the time. I gave her my condolences and my phone number. I also told her to call me if she needed someone to talk to or to help her. Eventually D.D. and I became good friends and developed a personal relationship. When I wanted to get things off my chest, I called her to talk.

One day we met at the Blue Chip Casino and I guess we were seen by one of Regina's friends because Regina came up to the casino, caught me red handed, snapped on me and D.D. Then Regina went outside after security asked her to leave and she put my Bentley on four flats. As Regina was getting away she was pulled over by the police and they tried to arrest her, but I refused to press charges on my girl. I could never do anything like that to her. Later the next day we made up and I was back to work.

In the meantime, Tension was invited to a competition in California hosted by B.E.T. As a result, I sent the whole "My Life Entertainment" crew and I stayed behind because I needed to make sure the insurance business was going well. Jazzy Pha and a few other celebs were there judging and once again Tension won that competition.

Tension called me and he was very excited while he was talking to Jazzy Pha and a representative of Grand Hustle. They were put on the phone to let me know how good the performance was by Tension. Later they all went out to a club, they were celebrating, having a good time, then a shootout broke out and Tension almost got shot. I felt so bad because normally I hired security for our crew at every city we visited. However, because I was not there, I forgot to hire them security.

Everyone came back home safe and it was business as usual. Later, I hired a Publicist for Tension that got him a meeting with Kevin Black, former Interscope Record Executive. Kevin was very interested in Tension, also known as "Mr. Gotdamitt." As a result, he made me an offer. I looked at the offer with my lawyer, "Hilal" who practiced in downtown Chicago and decided not to take the deal.

I was looking for a distribution deal for my Artist and the deal he offered was not a good one for "My Life Ent." at the time. Sometime later Michael Jackson's birthday was coming up and Prime Time asked me if Tension could close out the show. This was a good opportunity for Tension's career because people from all over the world would come and give tribute to Michael Jackson.

The tribute took place at the Jackson 5's old house located 2300 Jackson Street. People were coming and going, buying t-shirts, food and taking pictures at the house. Tension closed the performance out with "Mammay Doe." Everyone was singing the song along with Tension. After the performance Tension signed autographs and took pictures for hours. The video is on You Tube under "My Life Entertainment." I said to myself that my father "Mr. John Underwood" invested and helped the Jacksons in the beginning of their career; there it was his son was trying to create the next star from Gary by investing and helping him.

I realized that I am just like my father, a bona fide hustler. I am also like my mother because I have a love for people. I really love to be around people and that's why I like the entertainment industry.

Sometime afterwards I was in Mighty Sharp barbershop getting a haircut by my guy Arnell when I saw a young, up-and-coming boxer named Dangerous Don Moore. He was a close friend of Duke "I Got Next" Tanner, a successful boxer who is serving time in the Feds. Don told me he was being offered to be trained by Roger Mayweather and that he had the opportunity to fight on the under card when Floyd Mayweather was scheduled to fight.

Don told me he needed a management company like "My Life Entertainment" to help him with his career. Roger Mayweather would train Don, but he needed his expenses paid like housing and food, etc. That is where "My Life Entertainment" came in to help. Dangerous Don had a 21 wins - 0 losses boxing record, so I felt like he was worth the investment.

The next time I met with Don we signed a four-year deal and I flew him to Las Vegas to start training. I felt good about the deal we had because now I had two well-known talents from Gary that my company was promoting and managing.

The whole City of Gary saw what my company was doing and they happily supported the movement. In the meantime, Sean "Puffy" Combs, CEO of Bad Boy Records created a group called "Day 26." When Will, one of the members of the group came back home, he moved about five blocks away, in the subdivision where I lived.

I developed a good business relationship with Will by doing shows in Chicago and Gary. One show we did in Gary at the Link Bar on a Sunday, we promoted so well that the day of his show, I swear there were all females in the audience. I can count on my hand how many men came. I could not believe how many beautiful women came and supported Will. I learned that night as a promoter that I also needed to provide entertainment for the guys. It would have been nice to have brought some World Star Hip Hop Honeys to entertain the men and I would have had more people there. Will did a good job that night in front of the females and they all enjoyed themselves. After a few shows together, Will and I remained good friends.

A few weeks later "My Life Entertainment" promoted a show in Indianapolis featuring Jeezy as the headliner. I was so busy that I was not able to make it so I had "Lil Man" JTP Productions oversee the show. He also invested, to make the show a success.

After the show and after all the money was counted "Lil Man" could not come bring my share of the profits. Therefore he sent his girlfriend Latanza to bring me my half of the money which was $39,000. While she was traveling from Indianapolis she was pulled over and the state trooper smelled marijuana in the car. He searched the car, found a small roach, then he found the $39,000 in her purse. Latanza was questioned for hours and she kept telling them that it was show money she was bringing me. The State Trooper let her go and kept the money. Once I found out what happened I called the department where the Trooper worked and demanded my money. They didn't believe me, so they turned the money over to the F.B.I. and it stayed with them. I was upset but I kept it moving thinking about all the other obligations with "My Life Entertainment" that needed to be met and I just worked harder.

In the meantime, I was still doing shows with the World Star Models. At this time Platinum Dior was a Hood Star because of her World Star videos and I promoted two shows in one day with her. The first appearance was at the Link Bar and everyone in the city showed up. Tension and Thugged Out (Mutt and Jeff) performed.

Later that night we went to Adrianna's in Chicago where at least 700 people showed up to meet Platinum Dior in person. I drove my Arnage Bentley and I had my whole crew in a stretch limousine. Platinum took pictures with a lot of fans and she even signed autographs that night for many fans as well. I had my sister Angel out with us that night and my partner "Lil Man" fell in love with her at first sight. Once we were leaving after having a successful night we had a bottle of Grey Goose left and Platinum was carrying it to the car while I was getting money from the club owner, from the door sales.

An officer walked up to the Bentley while Platinum was in the passenger seat. When I walked toward the car to see what was going on with the Officer, he took the bottle from her hands and said that he was towing my Bentley because of an open bottle in my car. I laughed, thinking he was playing and told him that my company did business with the owner that night and we were just leaving to go back to Indiana. He told me with a hateful look on his face that I was not the boss and that he was the real boss. The officer took my keys in front of hundreds of people and told me I had to get my car back from the tow yard.

I was so upset that a tear flowed from my eyes. Both Platinum and I along with my sister Angel jumped in the stretch limo and came back with the whole crew. In that moment, I realized that we were making so much noise in the streets with the many things "My Life Entertainment" was doing that we even had the police hating on us. That's sad because my company was only promoting positive entertainment for our fans.

The next day I went to the tow yard to get my Bentley, paid $500 to the Manager and all he wanted to know is who I was. I could not believe they had my Bentley in the middle of so many junk cars. I gave the manager my card and I left. At the time, I had the whole "My Life" Crew staying at the Sybaris in Chicago. After being there for a few days I went back to my home to check on Regina. There was a card from the F.B.I. on my door, telling me to give them a call when I get a chance. I said to myself they must be ready to return my $39,000. Therefore I immediately called the Agent and he immediately picked up the telephone. He told me his name was "PB" and that he wanted to talk to me because I was the focus of a wire fraud investigation. I told him that since I was not under arrest he needed to contact my lawyer to set up the interview.

I gave him my lawyer's number and I hung up the phone. Before I hung up the phone all I heard was him on the other end laughing loudly. Then I said, "This must be a joke." So, I dismissed it in my mind, the whole conversation I had with him, but I did get a little paranoid. As a result, I packed up some things and moved to New Orleans with Platinum at the time. My intention was to live there for about three months but I got caught up. I had my nephew Jimmy run my insurance business and I had Lil Man manage Tension while I was busy doing shows with the models. I also hired a Manager from Minnesota to manage my boxer, Dangerous Don Moore when I was not available to negotiate deals for him.

While in New Orleans I made a big impression in the city. Some people recognized me from World Star and a lot of rappers would give me their CD to listen to in hopes of me investing in their career. New Orleans is a great big party city and my personality fit right in. I was everywhere things were happening and I also began promoting parties in that city as well. My Life Entertainment promoted one party for Platinum's birthday at "She She's" and it was a blast. Roxy Reynolds was there performing, looking very sexy and ready for whatever. The Ying Yang Twins also attended the party.

Juvenile from the Hot Boys Cash Money came and made an appearance as well as some local Artists that had music rotating on the radio. Platinum Dior was at the height of her career at the time and "My Life Entertainment" became an Underground King in the Hip Hop community. The video is on the internet under the name "Platinum Takeover." That night I was drinking and smoking Cush with a backpack full of money on my shoulder. The Ying Yang Twins, Roxy Reynolds, Juvenile and a few strippers were In the V.I.P. section. At that time, Juvenile and I became good friends.

Juvenile let me hear three songs he recorded, had the DJ play it and he asked me which one he should release as his first single. After hearing the songs, I chose "Power" and little did I know he would release the song later featuring Rick Ross "The Boss." That whole night was recorded, both Platinum and I were dressed to impress. Platinum had on her red bottoms and she was iced out in jewelry. I had on Gucci, wearing 100 karats in diamonds on my neck, wrist and hands. Everyone who attended the event ate very good and left "She She's" satisfied. After that show in New Orleans the whole city was trying to get at me to do business.

One of Master P and Bird Man Jewelers saw me in a club, gave me his card and told me to call him because I may be interested in a piece of jewelry he had. The next day I called the jeweler "Sol" and met with him. Then he pulled out a big charm in the shape of Louisiana. He told me it was the Hot Boy B.G. charm and he got it from B.G. before he went to the Feds. I bought the charm from "Sol" for ten thousand dollars and I vowed to give the charm back to B.G. when he got out. In the meantime, I was wearing the charm at different clubs in New Orleans. People would ask me if it was B.G.'s charm that I had on and I would tell them that I was holding it for him till he got out the Feds.

The city of New Orleans had a lot of love and respect for B.G. I noticed that Platinum was also loved and had a lot of respect from the city. I believe that was the reason no one tried to rob me while I was stunting in the city because of my connections with Platinum, B.G. and Juvenile. I still walked around with a .45 caliber everywhere I went to protect me from a hater who may want to try me. One day Platinum and I were outside of "Passions," I was outside my Range Rover talking to a guy about the music industry; then all of a sudden I heard two loud shots right at me.

I thought I got shot so I started running backwards with my .45 Glock out trying to aim in the direction of the shots. I jumped in the Range Rover and took off, but I still wonder if those shots were for me. There were rumors that someone was out to kill me in New Orleans because I was bringing too much attention to myself. After that experience, I never went back to Passions again.

Since "Mammay Doe" was kind of losing its buzz I decided to Executive Produce another song entitled, "My Life." I wanted to work with platinum selling Artists who were around my age at the time, because I wanted the song so be about "My Life Entertainment." I called Twister and set things up with his management team. After the paperwork and contracts were done my Producer and Engineer, J Trax sent them the track. I also called Juvenile personally and made arrangements with him. Since we were friends we did not use contracts to solidify the deal.

One day after I emailed the track to Juve he called me and told me to meet him at the studio. When I got there I noticed a brand new chopper in the front living room area and at the back there was a very nice studio where Juve made his music. Once Juve and I finished smoking a few joints he signaled me to come to the studio.

Now there I was in the booth with Juve standing in the back corner while he was just snapping on the track. I could not believe what I witnessed; Juve was free styling on the track; telling the story about "My Life" right off his head. Afterwards Juve's wife got us both some Popeyes chicken, we ate and talked.

I showed him all the videos "My Life Entertainment" had on the internet and we talked about doing business in the future since he had just gotten a deal from Cash Money again. He downloaded the master copy on CD and gave it to me. Then I left to go back to my other house in Metairie, Louisiana.

Sometime afterwards I went to visit my daughter, Mahiah. After spending the weekend with her, on the flight coming back I bumped into Christopher Williams from the movie, "New Jack City." He was also a popular recording Artist in the 90s. We both talked about our entertainment industry goals.

After I told him about my project with Juvenile and Twister he agreed to sing the "My Life" hook on the song. We exchanged telephone numbers and emails, then when I got back I emailed him the track. I did not know that he would take as long as he did to lay the track.

While I was waiting on Christopher Williams to finish I was in contact with Rawle, Twister's Manager, to get the masters of Twister's verse on the track. I had to get my Producer, J Trax to communicate with Rawle because for some reason we just did not get along. During a three-way telephone call with Christopher Williams, Rawle made me so mad that I snapped on him and hung up the telephone. The problem was that he wanted more money than what he agreed upon and I was not having it. I let my Producer handle it from then on and it was later resolved.

During that time, Regina would break up with me over just about anything, on a regular basis. Getting confused, I made an impulsive decision, Donisha "Platinum Dior" and I got married. I was smoking weed, partying and under so much stress that I was not thinking clearly. I am not saying that Platinum was a bad person.

I had known Regina so long and I loved her so long that I knew I was really supposed to marry her. However, Regina just didn't think I was really ready for marriage and she was right. Regina told me this after I gave her a $30,000 dollar ring. Her son Terry was with me when I bought it and he gave me his blessing.

Regina was waiting on me to change and at the same time she knew I loved her. In fact, the whole time I was living in New Orleans Regina waited for me while I was in my madness. Regina continued to keep her mind on her "Good Scents Oils" business that was doing very well online. One of her main customers was a boutique in Atlanta owned by Kandi Burruss from "Atlanta Housewives" and a member of XSCAPE. Regina focused on her business the whole time I was running wild in the entertainment business. She promoted a lot of videos online to promote "Good Scents Oils." She taught women how to smell good and sweet for their mate.

Regina captured a lot of followers because of her beauty, men and women love looking at her and hearing her talk.

In the meantime, Tension was doing features and I also sent him to Texas to appear in the "Rock and Roll" video of Thugged Out (Mutt and Jeff), featuring Gucci Mane. That video can also be seen on the internet under Dirty Game or Mutt and Jeff. I also continued doing shows in Chicago with a model named "Pinky." That business operation was successful at drawing big crowds which provided opportunities to cash in at the door of the clubs.

Back in New Orleans I had my old friend Bun-B do a show, drawing big crowds and big names like Mannie Fresh, etc. I was in the air flying more than I was on the ground, almost every couple of days I was flying first class Delta or American.

It had been a while since I saw Dangerous "Don" Moore, my boxer fighting in the Mayweather camp, so I decided to fly to Las Vegas with some of the "My Life" Crew and surprise him. When I arrived in Las Vegas with my crew we all stayed at Caesar's Palace. Every time I go to Vegas I stay at Caesar's Palace. I really liked the atmosphere there and I also loved the shopping. The last time I was in Las Vegas was the Billboard music awards and I had a seat right behind Usher watching Beyoncé perform the opening act.

After checking into Caesar's Palace I went to Mayweather's boxing gym and the only people there were Don's Fitness Trainer and a few other boxers. I filmed the inside of the gym and put it on Facebook letting everybody know where I was at the time. Don's Fitness Trainer along with Roger Mayweather, his Boxing Trainer invited me to a boxing match at the Bellagio that night where I was scheduled to meet with Floyd Mayweather after the fight and talk about getting Don a big fight soon. I got a chance to speak to Floyd Mayweather briefly but he was behind schedule and he had to go. Then I had a talk with Don's Strength and Conditioning Coach and Roger Mayweather to discuss Don's future in boxing for Floyd Mayweather's camp.

The Strength and Conditioning Coach said that they offered Don two fights, with Andre Dirrell and another big fighter whose name I can't remember. That was about two months prior to my visit, but Don turned down the offer. Immediately, I got kind of upset that he would turn down a fight without talking to me or the Manager I hired for him. However, I kept my composure and I told them I would get back to them soon because there was a misunderstanding.

I called Don and asked him about what his trainer was telling me. He told me that he was simply not ready to fight. I tried to convince him that he was ready because he had been training for at least a year and with a 21-0 record, that was enough time. I also questioned him, "You've been sparring with Floyd Mayweather, the greatest boxer in the world pound for pound for all that time and you're still not ready?" I eventually backed down, supported his decision and flew back to New Orleans.

In New Orleans I met up with Juvenile at his studio and I was telling him about my trip to Vegas while we smoked on a joint. Since I was from Gary, Indiana, all my associates and friends were miles away, so Juvenile was a friend to talk to since we were doing business together.

As soon as I told Juve that my fighter turned down two big fights that would have made him six figures, Juve immediately told me that Floyd must have took his confidence sparring with him on a regular basis. Juvenile told me to think about it, you've got your fighter sparring with Floyd Mayweather on the regular, each time Floyd beats him in the ring he loses more and more confidence. I was so high, but I felt what Juve told me because I could see with my mind's eye how that could happen to a boxer like Don. I never told Don what Juve told me, I just kept that truth to myself and hoped he would get his confidence back. As I was talking to Juve, I had an "Aha" moment and I realized that if I would have been in Vegas more in the gym with Don that would've helped his confidence when he sparred with Floyd.

Don was away from his family in a place where the only people he knew were the money team and he lacked the support from me. I thought paying for his living expenses while in Vegas was good enough, but I was wrong. Eventually, Don got a fight back home in Merrillville, Indiana at the Radisson. He won the fight unanimously, jabbing and punching the guy's lights out and that gave him his spark for boxing again.

While in New Orleans spending a lot of time gambling, I got a call from the radio station telling me that Rick Ross was in town shooting a video for the song "Hold Me Back" and they needed some girls to be in the video. I told them that was not a problem and I came to the set with my people to be in the video. Gunplay, Wale and Currency who is from New Orleans were all on the set. Before they started shooting the video I walked up to Rick Ross and he remembered me from the show he performed at the Diamond Center back in Gary. We both started talking about that night on stage with the Hennessey bottle smoking on a blunt. Then I told him I was living in New Orleans now operating the entertainment company. They wanted me to appear in the video, but everyone had to take their shirts off in the video. I had all my jewelry on, I was wearing Gucci, so I was fresh to death, but I also had a .45 Glock in my back waist area so I kept my shirt on to keep it concealed. I stood behind the cameras the whole time the video was shot.

I was laughing at Gunplay making faces at the camera taking his thumb across his nose multiple times. The kids behind Rick Ross and Gunplay play were just happy to be in a video. It really was a lot of fun to see so many people come to support us.

The day was peaceful with no fights or any arguments. For about six months straight, every week I was in a different city promoting a show with many Artists and Models. I eventually got a call again from one of the 106 & Park Executives wanting Tension to come back to the show and compete for a final showdown for $5,000 and a Coca Cola endorsement.

After agreeing to compete for the final showdown I called Tension; I told him what was up and to head straight to the studio to record a new song for the 106 & Park competition. The song he came up with was called "Let's Go" and it was designed to hype up all the kids that were watching. After mixing and the master of the song we sent it to the 106 & Park Executive to approve the song to be performed on the show. This song was approved, and I made arrangements for the whole "My Life" Crew to go to New York and shine representing Gary, Indiana. The competition was in about three weeks so I went back to Gary, spent some time with my family and everywhere we went everybody was congratulating us, wishing us good luck on us going back to 106 & Park to compete.

It felt good being back in Gary where I was born and raised getting respect from the whole city, driving around in my Arnage Bentley, throwing bags of single dollars in every hood in Gary. That weekend, Tension and I went to the Link Bar on a Saturday. I was smoking some Cush while Tension went inside the club.

I was planning on going in after I was finished, but I got so high that I could not get out of the car. I was just stuck in one position thinking about everything I had done in the last four years. Luckily, a young lady I know named D.D. (her first name is Devida) from East Chicago, now working in Gary as a beautician got in the Bentley and started talking to me, keeping my mind from deep thought and the high went down.

We drove around for about ten minutes and I pulled back up at the Link Bar to pick up Tension and went to take him home. D.D. had always been a positive person in my life. She always had good things to say about me and she always encouraged me to have success. She wished the whole "My Life" Crew success on 106 & Park.

The next day I flew out to Miami, Florida to a party that one of the Kardashian's was hosting. I got a chance to network there, pass out some business cards and get a few numbers. I shopped all through South Beach buying Gucci and Louis Vuitton, eating at the nicest restaurants and being chauffeured around in a limousine for two days. I spent some time with the friend I had a personal relationship with in Miami and I flew back to New Orleans to my second house afterwards.

I got back to my house and immediately Donisha "Platinum Dior" started arguing with me and throwing water on me while she was attacking me. My mom was calling me, so I answered and it was my brother, Pretty Ricky. He was visiting our mom at that time and I started telling him I was getting attacked by Platinum. He started yelling at me saying, "Pull the .45 Glock out" while my phone was on speaker. I guess she really thought I was going to pull a gun out on her, so she went outside and called the police. I was on the phone when the police came and they arrested me. Then they went up to my master bedroom, found my gun under my mattress, dismantled it and gave it to Donisha because in Louisiana a person didn't need a permit to carry a weapon.

Their laws are different from most states. The police took me down to the station, realized that they had no charges against me, but held me for 48 hours. I called Prime Time from jail and told him that I may not be able to make it to New York for the 106 & Park competition and that he may have to take the lead if I could not make it. However, I was released just in time before my flight to New York and I made it.

I was so happy I made it because I would have missed my daughter and one of the biggest highlights of "My Life Entertainment" history, performing a second time for live television at 106 & Park. Like I said, my daughter and my ex-wife, Vatina came to support. JTP Production was there; Prime Time and his dance crew came and performed on stage with Tension. He was the last act to perform and when Rocsi asked Tension who he was looking forward to doing music with, he said Rick Ross.

Tension went out and performed the song "Let's Go" and the crowd loved it. In fact, Tension was getting louder cheers from the audience than the other two acts. Sadly, Tension performed last and he ended up losing the competition.

I later learned that because he performed last, his votes did not totally get counted before the show ended and they had to give the title to the act with the most votes by the end of the show. As a result, the first act won the competition. I am not going to lie, my feelings were hurt and our whole crew was sad about the results. My daughter, Mahiah made me feel better just looking at her smile and listening to her tell me that we still are winners. Our crew still went out and celebrated the fact that Tension appeared on 106 & Park and performed.

The next day I took Mahiah shopping and spent time with her; we talked about meeting Tyra Banks at the 106 & Park green room. My daughter was excited to take pictures and see her. My daughter was happy to be in New York for the first time in her life. I made sure that Mahiah and her mom made their flight on time. I also made sure the crew made their flight on time. Then I finally made my flight back to New Orleans to my other house. Once I arrived, I got my clothes and my Bentley and moved into the Harrah's Casino Hotel for a few weeks. At that time, I was managing a model named Mamie, who did magazine shoots and some walk-thru events at a few clubs.

I eventually moved back to my house in Indiana and rekindled my relationship with Regina. I had a transport service bring my Range Rover back to Indiana as well. Regina waited for me patiently while I was in my madness and she continued to love me. I took a brief break from the industry to spend time with Regina. Both of us traveled to many places, attended Tyler Perry plays and went to a Mayweather fight in Vegas. Our next trip together was in South Carolina to support one of her Good Scents Oils Sales Reps.

On our way back to Indiana, Regina got a call from one of her neighbors saying that the Feds were at her house looking for me. They also told her they had a warrant for my arrest. I then remembered the phone call that I received some time back from an agent named Paul asking to interview me about some wire fraud transactions. As me and Regina approached Michigan City I got off the highway at the exit near a hospital. I gave Regina my phone, my jewelry, my credit cards and I told her that I would check myself into the hospital to stay there and handle all my business affairs before I turned myself in to the Officer. Paul and Detective Joe picked me up from the hospital and arrested me on the spot.

I was kind of confused because I was taken to the county jail and not the Fed building to be booked. I found out that the state was charging me, not the Feds and I was facing the maximum of three years in prison if found guilty. The prosecutor really had it out for me because she was being influenced by the Feds. It turned out that Mamie had cooperated with the Feds to help get me indicted because I had left the relationship.

The lawyer told me after a year that my only offer was a three-year plea or I could go to trial and take the chance of being found guilty on all counts and have a consecutive sentence given to me. Out of three years, I would only do 18 months, so I took the plea.

What I was charged with involved something that was done by a person that I was affiliated with and not by me. Since I owned the company and I was not about to snitch on anybody, I was the one who took the fall. The press, quite unfairly, reported zealously on the length of my sentence and went out of their way to make me look as bad as possible. I eventually went to prison, a lot of people and some of the guys from my city were surprised to see me there. I was like a prison celebrity because a lot of the guys were familiar with my work with the entertainment company.

I gained weight because everybody cooked for me, even the Mexicans. I lost a lot by going to prison; I breached the contract I had with Tension, Don and all the Models. My insurance agency American Freedom Financial LLC was also at a standstill. I was living in a tiny cell, thinking about where I went wrong. Then one month before I was released from the State, the Feds charged me with the same thing, Wire Fraud/Identity Theft.

I could not believe that I was charged again for the same exact crime. I learned later that the Federal Agent and another Detective just had it out for me because through their investigation they saw all the cars I was driving; the Bentley, Range Rover, 600 Mercedes, CTS Cadillac, the Honda Gold Wing, 750 BMW, Hummer and the 1974 Cadillac Eldorado.

They saw the mansion in Indiana and Louisiana that I was living in and they investigated how much I paid for all my jewelry. They knew all 27 countries I had traveled to, they followed me on Twitter, Facebook and Instagram. Because they knew all of that they became jealous and assumed that I got all my assets from some type of fraud. They realized later that I was just a businessman who made a mistake with some of my wire transfers.

They put a lot of man hours into investigating me, so they wanted me to get the most time possible, that's why the State charged me, then the Feds. The government didn't offer me a plea, the only option was to plea open to the Judge. They were hoping that the Judge would give me the max twelve years, but the Judge respected the fact that I was a businessman who just made a mistake with some of my transfers. As a result, he gave me 48 months.

The Federal Agent and the Detective who investigated me were very upset because they wanted me to get more time so they convinced my jeweler to file charges against me in Louisiana over a transaction that was returned, which was conducted on my behalf by one of my models. I had paid that jeweler a long time ago in cash for that deal.

I sent him ten thousand dollars in total, $4K for the return purchase and $6K for a new piece I bought from him. I paid him in cash and did not get a receipt, so he was able to get away with filing bogus charges against me, knowing he had been paid already. The Feds knew that with another charge on me while serving time I would not qualify for a halfway house or the year off for the RDAP Program. This too was designed to keep me in jail longer.

While in federal prison FMC Lexington I decided to get my life in order. I also found out that the Feds had obtained some of my files provided to them by Platinum Dior (Donisha). She felt scorned because I had left her and she thought I made her look crazy in her city. Later, however, she regretted what she had done.

I was upset at first, but I eventually forgave her because I realized that holding a grudge is like taking poison and expecting someone else to die. I started working on getting my body in shape and taking care of my health. I also started getting my mind together by reading books and studying the Bible again.

The few years I had been in prison I took a lot of programs where I learned and came to understand what relationships are and identify what makes them healthy or unhealthy.

I examined the positive qualities that lead to healthy relationships. I was able to explore the components of effective communication. While doing time I repaired my relationship with Regina, divorced Platinum Dior and I left behind the unhealthy ones. I was able to reflect on my actions while doing business in society and realized that I was addicted to the lifestyle of materialism such as gambling, eating and shopping.

I examined the cost and payoffs of these addictions and realized that it was not worth it, living a materialistic life. I explored the ripple effect of how my behavior affected everyone around me. Money and power made me feel grandiose and I felt that I could do whatever I wanted to do.

Thoughts control your feelings and behavior because when I was serving Jehovah my thoughts were spiritual, I only thought about advancing the Kingdom. After walking away from my relationship with God my thoughts were fleshly, all I wanted was more and more wealth and nothing was enough. I was never satisfied with anything because I didn't have real peace. But I learned to challenge my thinking because I can change my feelings and behavior.

I am the Master of my life and no other person or circumstance is. I began to break down the elements of physical health, evaluating my emotional well-being. I took the time to examine all my relationships in the past and present. I also took a look at the role that job satisfaction plays in a balanced lifestyle and also being involved in the community positively. As I reflected on my life I remembered the good that I was involved in before I took a bad course.

I remember giving a banquet style celebration for my mom and my ex-wife's mom, Ms. Colbert for raising their children with love and all the support they gave both of us. My mother was so happy that such an event was given for them.

I reflected on all the relationships I had been involved with in my life and I thank God for those experiences. I helped a stranger get her mother a pacemaker during my college years. I was a great father to my daughter, Mahiah. During the time I ran my insurance business I used my money to help a lot of people with their businesses and careers. I can think of many positive things I reflected on while being incarcerated in the Feds.

At the same time, I reflected on the negative things I did and how my decisions affected the people I love. I realized the mistakes I made and I learned very dearly from them. During my incarceration I was able to develop another book entitled "48 Laws of Sales" and "The Power of Perception." Throughout the years of my life as a Minister, Drug Dealer, Salesman and CEO, I developed a system of sales that if applied to your life any salesman can be successful. Showing personal interest to those I meet breaks down barriers when offering a product in sales.

Using illustrations and vivid hyperbole are also great tools to paint the picture in the mind of your potential clients. These are just some of the things I have learned that helped me make millions in the insurance industry and I will reveal all my secrets in the book "48 Laws of Sales." Hopefully, I can travel the states promoting my books and conducting seminars to instruct other salesmen on how they can maximize their potential and increase their sales.

At the age of 43 I am aware, finally, that I am here on earth to teach and help others. I realize that helping others gives me joy, peace and satisfaction. Being balanced is another important aspect of having success in life, because too much of anything is not good.

Since being incarcerated, I lost a lot of people to death that I was associated with in society. Mic-Check, "Q" from World Star Hip Hop, my cousin Andrea, Juble, my Aunt Elaine, my nephew Ray Ray, my Uncle June, my Uncle WL, Della and a few of my beloved cousins all passed away while I was incarcerated in the Feds. This is the only reason I regret the decisions I made going to prison. I was not able to be out and support their families as well as mine. Other than that, I can also say that this was the best thing to happen to me.

In the Bible there are many examples of men and women who were in a bad situation but later turned it into something positive, like Job; losing his family, getting sick, losing his wealth and all his friends but later gaining more than he ever had. Daniel was thrown into the lion's den and left for dead, but he survived unscathed. Joseph was sold into slavery, but later appointed by Pharaoh to be second in command over the entire land of Egypt, his house and his people. Jesus was put to death by men, was later resurrected and is now reigning as King in Heaven. I mentioned all these biblical examples to explain what I went through when I was thrown into prison.

I have come to understand that just like Daniel, Job, Joseph and Jesus came out victorious; I, Marlon L. Underwood will have the same results, being victorious at the end. I look back at my life, meditate on all my achievements and wonder if I can ever come back to top that kind of success. The knowledge I have acquired since I have been incarcerated tells me that it will happen as long as I believe and continue to speak it into existence. I learned that you are what you think. Everything that comes about in our life is brought about by our thinking. If you think bad thoughts, bad things come about in your life.

If you think positive and do positive things, the universe will return the positive back to you. Karma is a real law that all humans need to respect just like we respect the law of gravity every day. I have come to realize that there are many laws that exist for man to live by so that we can benefit from the blessings the Creator has in store for us. Some of these laws are the laws of attraction, the laws of love and the many laws or principles in God's Word, the Bible. By applying such laws or principles in our life it helps to enrich the quality of the life we have. Then you begin to shine as an illuminator in the world.

Another valuable thing that I did in prison was to take an honest look at myself to recognize and address my materialistic, impulsive lifestyle. During this process I learned that I first need to be adaptable because when negative events occur we are able to learn from them and move on with our lives. Sometimes when we are young we have experiences that we cannot shake, just like the death of my father and brother. The negative feelings that came with the loss pervaded my existence like a bad headache that comes about often and eventually interferes with my ability to have healthy relationships and successful careers.

For example, because of the loss of my father and brother I developed a fear of abandonment. Whenever things are not going right in my relationship and career I used the thinking error "cut off" to solve the issue. Technically, I just run away emotionally and physically from the situation to avoid any possible pain or hurt. First to get past repeating the same behavior "cut off", I learned to look back through my life and identify my early painful events that had a powerful impact on my world. I also started working out every day meditating on my life history. During that process I lost a lot of weight and got in great shape physically.

Then I began to release and eliminate old self-limiting beliefs. I started replacing them with empowering beliefs. Finally, I applied these techniques for anchoring positive new beliefs in my thought patterns so that it became second nature to think better. For example, just as millions of years ago an asteroid struck the earth and caused the death of the dinosaurs, the impact threw debris into the atmosphere like how an atomic bomb goes off darkening the skies and changing the climate causing the death of dinosaurs.

The impact of any trauma in our lives like death can have the same kind of effect on our outlook on life, darkening our perception which affects every aspect of our lives like our careers, marriage and relationships. These experiences will leave its mark and then be reactivated by events later in life that are similar to the early events; just like the sound of a motorcycle backfiring can trigger the traumatic memories of war. Having this understanding made me more balanced, bringing to balance my left and right side of my body; bringing to balance my goals as well as my mental, physical, external and internal as well as my past and future.

I realize now that remaining balanced is the key to success and happiness. When I see myself drifting I take the necessary measures to get back on track. How do I get back on track? Well, I examine myself such as my eating habits because what and how I eat makes a difference in how I think and feel on a daily basis.

Modestly eating nutritious healthy foods six times a day helped to keep my blood sugar regular, to keep my mood stable throughout the day, helping me to stay positive while being incarcerated. I also found that exercise is good for the body and mind to help keep me balanced throughout the day.

I can tell when I exercise that my brain releases chemicals (endorphins) that cause me to live with passion and my thinking abilities are very clear afterwards. Building a gratitude list daily helps me to stay more positive and focused on the good rather than the bad. Rather than looking for what's wrong, when you create a gratitude list you focus on the positive and it strengthens your awareness of what's more important in your life. Every day I was thankful for my life, my mother, my daughter, my girlfriend, my family, etc. Thinking about the things in life I am grateful for made me powerful in many ways that are hard to explain.

For example, "Why is it that a parent standing inside a crowded gym can pick out the sound of his or her child out of all the different sounds coming from 40 children in the gym?" It is because the parent is programmed to filter out all the voices of the other children as irrelevant. So, when we focus on the good and the things we are grateful for we begin to tune out the negative things as irrelevant. As a result, our brain processes the positive thoughts which will control how we feel. To a great extent, life is a self-fulfilling prophecy: what you focus on is what you get.

I also realize that renewal time is important, physical renewal; mental renewal; emotional renewal and spiritual renewal are four important aspects to staying balanced. <u>Physically</u> getting good sleep and good nutrition as well as good exercise is vital. <u>Mentally</u> clearing your mind and relaxing daily is vital. <u>Emotionally</u> spending time with people and enjoying them has a great effect on you as well. <u>Spiritual</u> renewal is a crucial aspect of balance for everyone. I have been able to connect to God which changed my outlook on life and I was inspired to write this book about my life.

As you can see by reading my book, I have rediscovered my connection to happiness. I experienced a full sense of connection with my true self, with others and with life while I was incarcerated. Life is similar to the bamboo tree. This tree doesn't grow out of the ground until after five years of watering and nurturing while underground. When it finally does come out of the ground after all of those years of watering and nurturing, it grows several feet per day! Sometimes in life it may seem as though things are not moving for you fast enough. Then there may be times when it seems like you are not having success in business or you may even be incarcerated for many years. However, I encourage you to continue to water and nurture your life with knowledge and positivity. Never stop, because eventually when the time comes you will come out from the bottom of whatever situation you are in and grow – every single day – in ways that no one else around you is growing. Just like that remarkable bamboo tree.

Epilogue

These days I am involved with helping others to succeed in their careers, as well as social causes that I firmly believe in and care about deeply. Currently, I am accepting bookings to do motivational speaking. My primary topic is "How to be Successful in Any Kind of Sales Job." Sharing my many years of experience as a leading sales professional, I teach and share with my listeners "The 48 Laws of Sales" system that I created. This unique approach will help anyone make millions in any sales job under my Millionaire Mind Consulting Business. With the right skills, information and a positive frame of mind, a sales career can become the road to riches for those who want to achieve greatness. Helping people follow their dreams is now one of my main goals in life.

I am also involved with Prison Reform, having seen first-hand how the system works. I am in the process of forming an association called the United Prisoner Association to fight against unjust, excessively lengthy prison sentences for non-violent offenders.

This includes well-known cases like Chris Young (Soulja) and Duke "I Got Next" Tanner, along with countless others whose names the public are not familiar with, but whose voices so desperately need to be heard.

Finally, My Life Entertainment will always be my passion and my hobby, so I will always be involved with doing shows, looking for talent and management in the Entertainment Industry. For booking and contact information, please use the following address: mylifeent333@gmail.com

And as always:

Love, Life, Loyalty and Peace!!!

www.ingramcontent.com/pod-product-compliance
Lightning Source LLC
Chambersburg PA
CBHW022107160426
43198CB00008B/378